For Sayla and Sasha, may the reverberation of Black excellence
fuel every step you forge as you create your legacy.

To the branches of my family tree.
Mom, Dad, Scott, Anji, Mason, Dorian, and Julian—thank you. —S.W.

To Zöe —T.E.

The illustrations in this book were created with mixed media,
which includes acrylics, oils, printmaking, and collage on paper and wood.

Cataloging-in-Publication Data has been applied for and may be obtained from the Library of Congress.

ISBN 978-1-4197-4875-2

Text and illustrations copyright © 2021 Schele Williams • Book design by Pamela Notarantonio and Heather Kelly

Printed and bound in China • 10 9 8 7 6 5 4 3 2 1

Abrams Books for Young Readers are available at special discounts when purchased in quantity
for premiums and promotions as well as fundraising or educational use.
Special editions can also be created to specification.
For details, contact specialsales@abramsbooks.com or the address below.

Abrams® is a registered trademark of Harry N. Abrams, Inc.

ABRAMS The Art of Books
195 Broadway, New York, NY 10007
abramsbooks.com

YOUR LEGACY

A BOLD RECLAIMING OF OUR ENSLAVED HISTORY

written by
SCHELE WILLIAMS

illustrated by
TONYA ENGEL

Abrams Books for Young Readers
New York

YOUR STORY BEGINS IN AFRICA.

Did you know Africans were the first people on the earth? Africa is a continent that is home to many countries and many thriving nations.

For thousands of years, Africans cultivated their land and grew many kingdoms that were passed down from generation to generation. They dreamt of the day their land would be passed down to you.

African people had great pride in their heritage and culture. Each nation spoke its own language and had its own identity and talents.

They believed their skin was kissed by the sun and made many colors of brown to reflect all the beauty of the earth.

AS-SALAMU ALAYKUM!

SAWUBONA!

In the summer of 1619, ships from Europe arrived on the shores of Africa. European slave traders had come to take African people away. Although your ancestors did not want to leave their homes, they had no choice.

All the people taken were put on ships for a very long journey. They had no idea where they were going, and they feared what life was going to be like in this new place. But your ancestors were determined to survive.

When they finally landed in the Americas, they were surrounded by people from other African countries and Caribbean Islands. All of these people were now called slaves.

Your ancestors were immediately separated from one another and given new names. They were put into groups with other enslaved people, who all spoke different languages. They were forced to do grueling work.

Although they were strangers, they chose to

LOVE

and protect one another as family.

They needed to find a way to communicate with one another. It was their

INTELLECT

that allowed them to combine all the languages they spoke to create a new one, called Pidgin.

They also found a new language they could share . . . MUSIC.

Music was more than a language; it was a connection to Africa.
Your ancestors sang songs from their homeland to hold on to their
cultures and religions. They sang spirituals as prayers to help them survive.
Their bodies became drums as they stomped and clapped rhythms that
connected them to their past. Music was a powerful tool for survival;
it also became a powerful tool for escape.

For some enslaved people, escaping meant secretly learning to read and write in English, sneaking food and spices from the kitchen to cook something special, or smuggling messages to someone they loved. Those actions were important, for every act of defiance was empowering and

COURAGEOUS.

Sometimes, escaping meant running away.
Your ancestors wanted to be free again and to be
reunited with their families more than anything.
They wrote and sang songs with secret codes.

Some songs were used to help them find family members. Others were used to discuss plans to escape or to help others on their escape routes to freedom.

DETERMINATION

It was your ancestors' to survive that drove them to keep seeking ways to escape slavery, even though it was dangerous.

1. **HARRIET TUBMAN** was an escaped slave who led more than three hundred people to their freedom as conductor of the Underground Railroad.

2. **HENRY "BOX" BROWN** shipped himself in a wooden container from Virginia to Philadelphia.

3. **WILLIAM AND ELLEN CRAFT** boarded a train in North Carolina and escaped to the North. Ellen had light skin, so she cut her hair short and dressed in men's clothing. She wrapped her head in bandages to look like an injured white man. William pretended to be her servant.

4. FREDERICK DOUGLASS disguised himself in a sailor's uniform and carried a free sailor's protection pass loaned to him by someone who thought he deserved freedom.

5. ROBERT SMALLS worked on a steamer. When the white crew went ashore, Robert and the other slaves working on the ship took the boat and picked up their families at a special meeting place in the middle of the night. Robert put on the captain's uniform and sailed them all to freedom.

Your ancestors were brilliant.
They invented all kinds of amazing things.

JO ANDERSON—the reaper (a wheat harvester)

NATHAN "NEAREST" GREEN—master distiller

HENRY BOYD—corded bed frame, called the Boyd Bedstead

BENJAMIN BRADLEY—steam engine large enough
to drive the first steam-powered warship

BENJAMIN MONTGOMERY—steamboat propeller

NED—cotton scraper

But they were not allowed to put their names on any of their inventions or to
be paid for anything they created. Other people took credit for your ancestors'
work and made fortunes. They passed down your inheritance to their families.

JO ANDERSON

NATHAN "NEAREST" GREEN

BENJAMIN BRADLEY

HENRY BOYD

BENJAMIN MONTGOMERY

NED

But they could not pass down

BRILLIANCE.

That is **your** birthright.

That innovation has never stopped. Look around and feel proud knowing that it was the

STRENGTH,

hard work, and

INGENUITY

of your enslaved ancestors that built and continues to define America.
You are a part of that.

1. Blood plasma bank—Charles Drew

2. Automatic brake for trains—Granville T. Woods

3. Peanut butter—George Washington Carver

4. Black hair care empire—Madam C. J. Walker

5. Ironing Board—Sarah Boone

6. Jazz—Buddy Bolden, Bessie Smith, Duke Ellington, Dizzy Gillespie, Billie Holiday, Count Basie, Miles Davis, Ella Fitzgerald, and many more

7. Ice Cream—Augustus Jackson

8. Mailbox—Philip B. Downing

9. Carbon filaments for light bulbs, also involved in invention of the telephone—Lewis Latimer

Your ancestors never forgot who they were and where they came from. They walked with

GRACE and
DIGNITY.

Their names match the many gifts they have given to you.

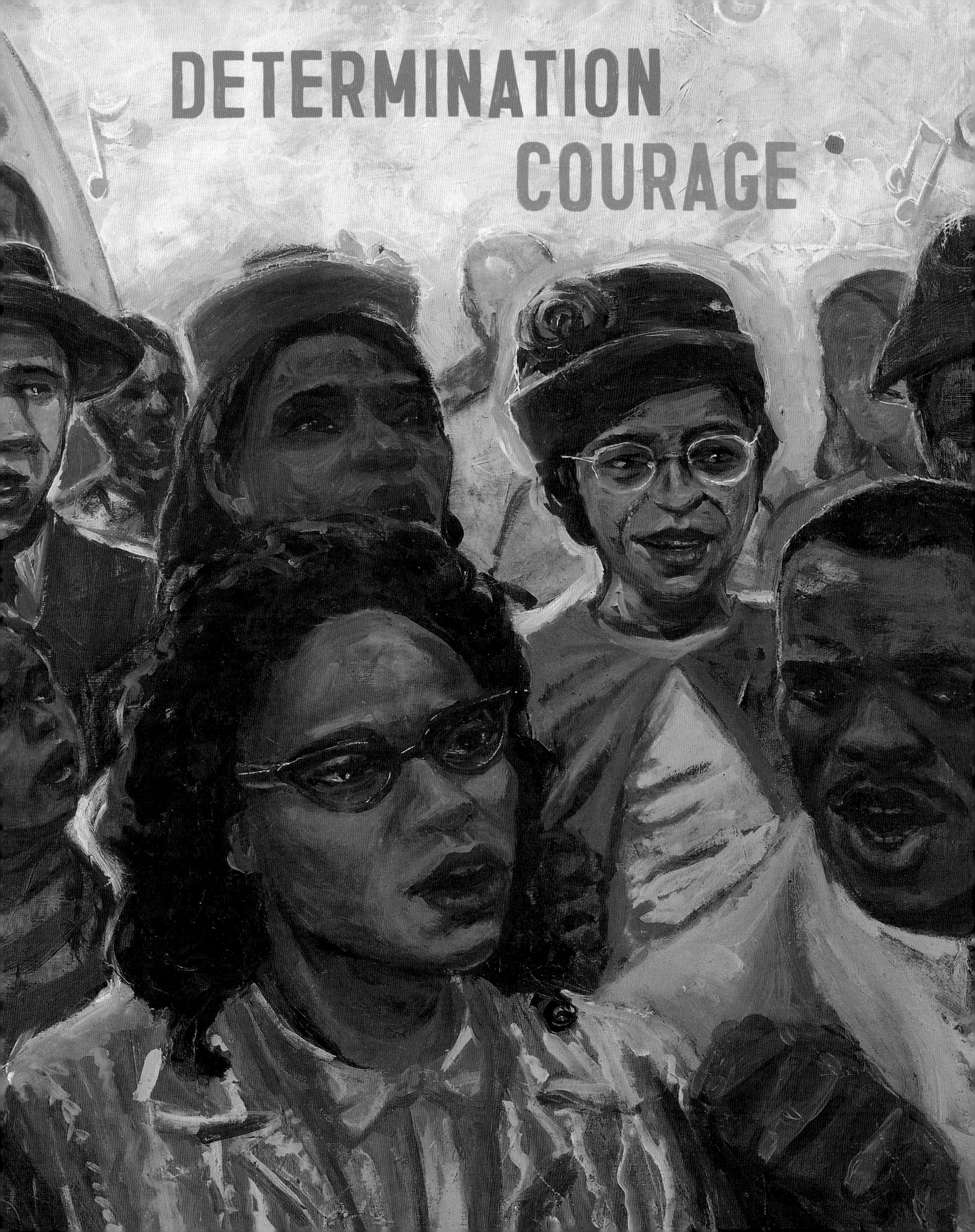
DETERMINATION
COURAGE

BRILLIANCE

MAYA ANGELOU

MUHAMMAD ALI

JAMES
BALDWIN

MARY MCLEOD BETHUNE

DIGNITY

INGENUITY

JOSEPHINE
BAKER

MISTY
COPELAND

ARETHA FRANKLIN

MILES DAVIS

MARIAN
ANDERSON

ALVIN AILEY

GRACE

COUNT
BASIE

ELLA FITZGERALD

Your ancestors passed down
the best of themselves.
That is your legacy.

All those years ago, they endured
so that you wouldn't have to. They
fought for their freedom and yours.

They knew that freedom
was the first step to equality.
They have given you all the tools
you need to grow the hearts and
minds of every nation.

EQUALITY is the gift you will
pass down to the next generation.

Now take a deep breath, close your eyes,
and receive your ancestors:

LOVE, INTELLECT, DETERMINATION, COURAGE, **BRILLIANCE, STRENGTH, INGENUITY, GRACE,** and DIGNITY.

They are a part of you.
Honor them and their sacrifices.

You are meant to do great things.
Walk tall, hold your head high,
and change the world.

AUTHOR'S NOTE

I wrote this book with humility and gratitude for the sacrifices made by my enslaved ancestors.

My name is Schele Williams. I am an African American woman and mother of two vibrant and amazing daughters, Sayla and Sasha. Their story began so differently than mine.

Unlike me, growing up in the 1970s, my girls have an expectation to see themselves in animated movies, on TV, and especially in books. They are curious and fearless, asking questions I never dared to ask. They want to know their story, and I want to be the one to tell them.

I've been a storyteller all my life. As a young adult, I was an actress on Broadway. In my thirties, I became a director and have directed productions all over the world. When I became a mom, I became a different kind of storyteller. I was very aware that I was curating my daughters' lives. My choices about art, music, dance, and literature would shape the lens through which my African American/White Jewish daughters would see themselves. I have consciously and deliberately vetted stories I was told as a child to ensure I am passing down to my children more complete versions of the ones I was taught. If you ask my eight-year-old daughter, Sasha, or my nine-year-old daughter, Sayla, who George Washington is, they will tell you he was a slave owner who signed the Fugitive Slave Act of 1793, and he was also the first president of the United States.

As a child, whenever I saw pictures of enslaved people in school, I felt ashamed. It was hard to see my people in chains with lash marks on their backs, speaking broken English, and dressed in rags. I was embarrassed, especially as one of only three Black children in my class. When I was older, I spoke to friends who'd had the same experience.

In high school, I remember we had to make a family tree as a class assignment. As I began drawing my tree and filling it in, I quickly realized I could only go back four generations and then . . . nothing. My family tree looked so small compared to my classmates'. Just empty lines where names should be. I desperately wanted to know the names of those who sacrificed so much for me. I longed for that connection. I needed to name them.

As I got older, the more I learned about slavery, the more I realized our history books barely scratched the surface of what happened to enslaved Africans and who they were. Our history books failed *all of us*. They never told us that enslaved people spoke broken English because they weren't allowed to speak their native languages or to have a formal education in America. They never told us that enslaved Africans wore rags because those were often the only clothes they were given, and that they weren't paid for the grueling work they did every day. They never told us that the lash marks on their backs were because of cruelty, not because of anything they did. And they certainly did not honor the ingenuity, intelligence, suffering, and perseverance of the men, women, and children they called slaves. I can't imagine how differently I would have seen myself in the world if I had learned that as a child.

I want African American families to have boldness and pride when telling our stories. The question for me became not *When are my kids ready to hear about slavery?*, but *How will I tell them?* How could I ensure that my children would not have the same experience I had when I first learned of slavery in school? When the time felt right for me to educate my own daughters, I decided I needed some guidance. Thus began my quest for a children's book about slavery that would empower its descendants with the truth.

I couldn't find it, so I wrote it.

Very quickly, I realized I did not want to write a book about slavery. I wanted to write a book about the enduring spirit of the enslaved. That distinction informed how I've chosen to introduce this complicated history to my children.

As I began writing this book, I didn't realize how much I needed it. How much I needed to name, celebrate, and acknowledge my ancestors out loud. I think of this book not only as a children's book, but a book to heal multiple generations of African Americans at the same time.

There is obviously so much more to tell, and many details to fill in as our kids get older, but I hope this book gives the reader the words to begin a lifelong conversation about our past as we look toward the future. I want every adult and every child who reads this book to feel proud knowing they come from a legacy of LOVE, INTELLECT, DETERMINATION, COURAGE, BRILLIANCE, STRENGTH, INGENUITY, GRACE, and DIGNITY. These are the names I have given my ancestors.

Much love and gratitude to my beloved legacy hive: Scott, Cait, Chris, Anji, Michael, Renée, Crystal, Daniel, Brandon, Suzanne, Bryan, Audra, LaChanze, Tom, Emma, Courtney, Joe, Julia, Steve, Cynthia, Bob, Austin, Holly, Lisa, Gabrielle and Dwyane. Special thanks to Tonya for creating a beautiful world for our ancestors to inhabit on every page.

Schele Williams

ILLUSTRATOR'S NOTE

I am deeply honored to have had the experience of illustrating this book! For me, not only was it an opportunity to share the journey of our ancestors who have paved the way for us, but it was also an opportunity to help pass along an important part of our past for the children, our future, in a way that we've never seen before!

Schele Williams has done an amazing job skillfully weaving together the vast tale encompassing over 400 years of the African American experience, creating beautiful imagery with her words. My job was made easy. For me, in illustrating this book, it was important to create imagery with rhythm—paintings that move and dance and never stay still, like a jazz song, so that the world may see with their own eyes as well as get an emotional sense of experiences our history books rarely discussed.

The sheer fact that this book can exist—written and illustrated by two Black women, people who were not considered citizens or even human, but property, only 400 years ago—speaks volumes. The fact that I would not be here to celebrate such an accomplishment were it not for their struggle speaks volumes. With this book, I hope to say thank you for the will and the determination, resilience, dignity, strength, sacrifice and perseverance of our ancestors. I hope I've done you all proud.

Tonya Engel